ASIA

THE GOBI DESERT

CHINA

Kan-Chow

Kashgar

Kain-du
Karazan •*Yachi*
Mien KARAIAN

KASHMIR
shawar

BURMA

INDIA

A Ladybird Book
Series 561

Marco Polo was one of the great travellers of all time and almost the first man from Europe to see the wonderful world of East Asia. He returned to write the story of his travels, something of which you can read in this book.

THE STORY OF
MARCO POLO

by L. DU GARDE PEACH, M.A., Ph.D., D.Litt.

with illustrations by JOHN KENNEY

Publishers: Wills & Hepworth Ltd., Loughborough

First published 1962   ©   *Printed in England*

MARCO POLO

Marco Polo was born in Venice in the year 1254.

Seven hundred years ago travelling about the world was very much more dangerous and difficult than it is to-day, and people who lived in Europe knew little or nothing about those who lived on the other side of the world.

From time to time ships came to Venice bringing silks and spices and strange jewels from the Far East. But the goods had been passed from one country to another, and had often taken years on the way. The sailors who brought them the last few hundred miles could tell nothing of the lands from which the silks and jewels had originally come.

In the warehouses at Venice the bales and boxes were piled high. Little Marco Polo, whose father was a merchant, often stared at the queer Chinese or Arabic writing with which they were marked, and wondered from what strange far-off places they had come.

Marco's father, Nicolo Polo, owned a house at a place called Sudak in the Crimea. He used to go there to collect the merchandise which had been brought from the East over a trade route called the Silk Road.

When Marco was six years old, his father Nicolo and his uncle Maffeo set off for Sudak. Marco waved good-bye to them on the quay by the Doge's Palace, and returned home with his mother.

The journey to Sudak and back took many weeks in those times. As the weeks and months passed, Marco began to look out eagerly for the return of his father and uncle, and the presents they would be sure to bring him.

But the months became years and little Marco could hardly remember what his father looked like. His mother died, and Marco went to live with other relatives.

Then one day, in 1269, a ship sailed into the harbour from Constantinople. Aboard it were Nicolo and Maffeo.

Marco was now a big boy of fifteen. Excitedly he listened, during the days which followed, to his father's stories of the strange countries he had visited.

Nicolo Polo and his brother Maffeo had not remained at Sudak. Whilst they were there, they had met some Russian merchants, who had told them of good trading to be done further east.

They reached a place called Bokhara on the eastern side of the Caspian Sea, and from there they intended to return home. But there was fighting in Persia, and the roads were unsafe. So instead of returning, the two Venetian merchants decided it would be safer to continue eastwards in the company of some Chinese merchants.

At last they came to China. The capital of China, Pekin, was many hundreds of miles from Bokhara, and no people from Europe had ever been there.

Nicolo and Maffeo Polo were kindly received in Pekin by the Emperor, Kubla Khan. He listened with interest to all they told him about the way people lived in the Western World.

Kubla Khan heard about Christianity for the first time, and he asked Nicolo Polo to return to Venice and bring back some Christian monks. Perhaps Kubla Khan hoped that they would convert the Chinese people to Christianity.

By the time Nicolo and Maffeo were ready to start on the long return journey to Pekin, Marco was seventeen. They decided to take him with them.

It was in the year 1271 that Marco Polo went aboard a little ship in the harbour at Venice. It was the beginning of a journey lasting three and-a-half years, which was to make him one of the most famous travellers in the world.

From Venice they sailed down the Mediterranean to Acre, and then went overland to Jerusalem.

At Acre, Nicolo, together with Maffeo and Marco, met a priest called Theobald, who afterwards became Pope Gregory X.

Nicolo told Theobald about his previous journey to China, and how the Emperor Kubla Khan had asked that they should return, bringing with them priests who would preach Christianity to his subjects. Theobald promised to find two monks who would be willing to face any hardships or dangers in the service of the Church.

The three Venetians were now ready to start on the long overland journey across Asia.

In the Church of the Holy Sepulchre at Jerusalem, there was a lamp which had been burning without ever going out for more than a thousand years. Nicolo wished to take some of the oil from this lamp, and with it to light the lamp of Christianity in China. His wish was granted, and the party of five men sailed up the coast to Layas, a city with a trade in spices and cloth of gold, from which merchants travelling to the East usually started.

From Layas the road lay eastwards across Persia.

It was not what we to-day would call a road. It was rough, sometimes becoming a mere track across desert sands and very difficult to follow. Rivers had to be forded, and often the way led along narrow ledges cut in the side of precipitous cliffs. Far below, in deep, rocky gorges, were dangerous rapids.

The thought of this difficult road filled the two monks with fear, and when they met a party of armed men who told them there was fighting going on in Persia between the army of the King of Egypt and an invading army of Mongols, they refused to go any further. So the three Venetians set off alone.

They travelled sometimes on foot, sometimes on mules or camels, and camped at night under the stars. Marco must have felt a long way from his comfortable home in Venice.

Marco was now in country such as he had never seen before. Fortunately he took very careful note of everything he saw on the way.

One of the strange sights which he remembered was a fountain of oil which came up out of the earth. The people who lived there told him that it never stopped, day or night. They used the oil to burn in their lamps or to rub on their sick camels.

This place has since been developed, and is now known as the Baku oil-fields, from which come millions of gallons of oil every year. This oil is converted into petrol to drive the cars and aeroplanes which to-day cover the world.

Marco also listened to many stories and local legends, which he afterwards wrote down. One of these was about Noah's Ark, which, he was told, was still to be seen on the top of a high mountain, Mount Ararat, where it had landed after the Flood.

The three travellers now turned south, making for the Persian Gulf, where they hoped to find a ship to take them round India, on the way to China. By going by sea they would avoid crossing the dangerous Gobi desert.

They were travelling only about twenty miles a day, as the road was very bad, and the very hot weather meant that they had to rest for three or four hours in the middle of each day.

After many days they came to the famous city of Baghdad, which Marco describes as "the noblest and most extensive city to be found in this part of the world."

Baghdad was famous for velvet and cloth of gold and rich brocades, which no doubt interested the merchants from Venice. It was also the city of Harun-al-Raschid and the Arabian Nights. When Marco visited it, it was splendid with brightly tiled mosques and minarets, surrounded by groves of palm trees and beautiful gardens.

The town towards which Marco and his father and uncle were going was called Kerman.

They had crossed the plains of northern Persia without meeting with any of the armed men who were said to be fighting in the area, the rumour of which had caused the two monks to turn back.

In fact the journey had become a very pleasant one. They had travelled with a number of other merchants, together with their slaves and guards. These caravans, as they were called, often consisted of hundreds of camels and many hundreds of men. In this part of the world, where robbers and bandits were often met, this was safer than travelling alone.

The road was not always through deserts or over high, dangerous passes. There were regions of rich country pastures, and even in the deserts there were oases of palm trees. Marco tells of hunting and hawking during this part of the journey.

At Kerman the road forked. Travellers to the East either took the northern route, to the north of Afghanistan, or turned south to a port at the end of the Persian Gulf, called Ormuz.

The southern road, which Marco now travelled, was through very wild and mountainous country. On a mountain pass, ten thousand feet high, he suffered from the intense cold, only to descend to a stiflingly hot plain.

Here the party of merchants was attacked by bandits.

There was a battle between the guards, who were with the caravan of merchants, and the bandits. But the guards were few, and if it had not been for the nearby castle of Konsalmi, to which they went for safety, Marco would have been killed or taken prisoner and sold into slavery.

However, the bandits soon rode off, and Marco journeyed on to Ormuz.

Ormuz was reached without any further dangers being encountered, and Marco, with his father and uncle, went to the quay to look for a ship.

They were not able to find one suitable for the long voyage round the south of India. Marco describes the ships at Ormuz as "of the worst kind, and dangerous for navigation."

He tells of the way they were built. No nails were used because the wood was so hard and brittle that it cracked like earthenware if a nail was driven into it. The planks were fastened by wooden pins and bound with ropes made of the husks of coconuts.

These ships had only one sail and no anchor, and in bad weather they were often driven ashore and wrecked.

Nicolo decided that it would be safer to return to Kerman and take the overland road to China.

It was with mixed feelings that they set out on the two hundred mile journey back to Kerman. They remembered the cold of the mountain passes and the heat of the plains. But most of all, they remembered the bandits.

They travelled cautiously, and managed to reach Kerman safely. From here they again set off eastwards.

The country which they now had to cross was naked desert. There was nothing but sand, neither trees nor water, and the heat was intense. Even wild animals avoided it.

Carrying water and food, Marco tells of the many days they spent crossing this desert, coming at last to the town of Balkh.

Here again the road divided. One way went north to Samarkand, another south via Kabul and Peshawar, and a third north-west through Bokhara.

But, after talking with camel-drivers, Nicolo decided to travel due east to Kashgar.

This was a shorter way, but it meant that they would have to cross some high and very mountainous country known as the "Roof of the World."

This was more difficult country than any across which they had so far travelled, and Marco tells of the hardships they experienced in climbing to this high tableland. When they reached it, they found a wide plain, covered with trees and grass. It was watered by pleasant streams, filled with fish, which they were able to catch for food.

When they came to cook the fish which they had caught, Marco was surprised to find that, in his own words, "however extraordinary it may be thought, from the keenness of the air, fires when lighted do not give the same heat as in lower situations, nor produce the same effect in dressing victuals."

We know to-day that water boils at a lower temperature the higher you get above sea level, because the air is thinner.

Marco then crossed the northern end of Kashmir, one of the most beautiful countries in the world. The town of Kashgar had beautiful gardens and vineyards; but then the scene changed and the travellers were confronted with the great Gobi desert, which would take them more than a month to cross.

It was a grim and forbidding place, with no life at all, except for an occasional oasis. Marco says of it: "It is a well-known fact that this desert is the abode of evil spirits, which lure travellers to their destruction. Losing the right path, and not knowing how to get back to it, they perish miserably of hunger."

Marco also saw the strange mirage of the desert. When one sees a mirage, lakes and trees and even buildings seem to appear in the midst of the sands. This is because the light from real buildings, trees and other objects (which are much further on and below the horizon), has been reflected by a layer of hot air.

Marco was glad to leave the desert behind, to see green fields and fertile valleys, and to be once again among the habitations of men. Here they were all received hospitably with singing and feasting, before going on their way once more.

Soon the party reached the Chinese town of Kan-Chow, where Marco must have had his first sight of the Great Wall of China.

This Wall is one of the wonders of the world. It was built more than two thousand years ago and its purpose was to keep the northern barbarians out of China.

It still stands to-day, 1400 miles long, through valleys and over mountains. Originally it was twenty feet high, and so thick that two carriages could drive side by side along the top of it. At short intervals were strong towers from which soldiers guarded the frontier.

It is strange that Marco Polo, who mentions so many things, says nothing about the Great Wall.

After resting at Kan-Chow, the travellers turned north-east, and whilst still forty days journey from Pekin, they were met by messengers from Kubla Khan.

There were, of course, no telephones in those days, but the Chinese had a system of carrying messages which was very well planned.

Stations were set up about twenty miles apart, with men and horses always on duty. When an important letter had to be carried over hundreds, sometimes thousands of miles, it was carried from one station to another, day and night, like a relay race.

So that there should be no delay, the horses all had bells on their harness. When he heard the sound of these bells coming along the road, the man at the next station mounted his horse ready to gallop off at once.

In this way a message could be carried four or five hundred miles in a day.

By means of this system of relays of messengers, the Emperor, Kubla Khan, had heard of the approach of the Venetians, even though they still had to travel for about forty days before they arrived at his Palace.

The next forty days were, however, very different from the hard, grim weeks in the desert. The travellers were now under the Emperor's protection, honoured guests to be everywhere received with respect and afforded every comfort and protection.

When they arrived at the Shandu, the wonderful Summer Palace of the great Emperor, they found that it was built of marble, and the halls and rooms were decorated with gold. The brilliant silken robes of the Emperor and his courtiers must have been a wonderful sight in this glittering interior, as the three travellers approached the throne.

Kubla Khan already knew Nicolo and Maffeo Polo. Now he looked for the first time on Marco Polo, who was to do him great services in the years to come.

The journey from Venice to China had taken more than three years. From time to time, Nicolo and Maffeo Polo and young Marco with them, had remained for weeks or months in towns where they had been able to carry on their business as merchants.

Marco was now a young man of twenty, and he was received with great favour by Kubla Khan. He remained for some months at the Summer Palace, and took part in the hunting expeditions which were the Emperor's favourite amusement.

Marco Polo describes the travelling pavilion carried on the backs of four elephants, in which the Emperor followed the hunt. It was made of wood, handsomely carved, the inside being lined with cloth of gold, and the outside covered with skins of lions.

Leopards, cheetahs, and even lions were trained to hunt down the game, and many thousands of huntsmen and soldiers accompanied the Emperor. When they camped for the night, the collection of tents and pavilions was described by Marco as like a populous city.

The capital of China, Pekin, was called Kanbalu, or Tai-du, when Marco Polo went there in the train of the Emperor, Kubla Khan.

It was a very wonderful city, built in the form of a square, each side of which was six miles long. It was surrounded by a high wall, with twelve gates and many towers, and each gate was guarded by a thousand soldiers. Inside the wall, the streets were laid out in long straight lines, crossing one another at right angles.

In the centre of the city there was a great bell, which was tolled every night. After the third stroke of the bell no-one was allowed to go about the streets, except on urgent business.

Kubla Khan's Palace was raised high above the town, with golden tiles on the roof, and the inside decorated with painted and gilded carvings. In the great banqueting hall six thousand guests could sit down to dinner at the same time.

Marco Polo was soon taken into the service of the State. He was high in favour with the Emperor, who quickly realised that he was honest and trustworthy.

He was also diligent and hard-working, and set himself to learn the four principal languages of China. As a result, he was employed by the Emperor on important affairs of state.

After only a very few years Marco Polo, a young foreigner of under thirty, was made Governor of Yan-gui. This was because Kubla Khan thought that a foreigner would not have friends and relations in China, and would therefore be fair to everybody.

For three years Marco Polo ruled in the name of the Emperor. Among many other things, he tells us of the printed paper money, made from the bark of mulberry trees, which the Chinese were using hundreds of years before it was introduced into Western Europe. These paper notes were stamped with the royal seal in red ink, and could be used anywhere in the Chinese Empire.

After serving as Governor of Yan-gui for three years, Marco Polo was so trusted by the Emperor that he was sent on important business to parts of China many hundreds of miles from Pekin.

One of these journeys took him to what we to-day call Burma. He was three-and-a-half months on the way, travelling in great state, with soldiers and servants, as the Emperor's representative, and visiting places with wonderful names such as Karazan, Kain-du, and Yachi, the chief town of Karaian.

At last he reached a city called Mien. Here he describes a wonderful tomb, consisting of two pyramids, one of which was covered with silver and the other of gold an inch in thickness. On the top of each was a golden ball, surrounded by little bells, which rang every time the wind blew.

On other journeys he travelled far to the north, where he tells of snow and ice, and of people dressed in skins, travelling on sledges.

After seventeen years in China, Marco Polo had become a rich man, and he began to think of returning to Venice. Kubla Khan was growing old, and Marco was afraid of what might happen to him if the Emperor was to die.

Nicolo and Maffeo were also growing old. They, too, had become successful in China and now wished to spend the rest of their lives in their own country.

Kubla Khan was reluctant to let them go. Marco Polo had become too useful as his most trusted servant. Then it chanced that a Chinese princess was preparing to travel by sea to Hormuz, to marry the King of Persia.

The ambassadors who had come to conduct her asked that the three Venetians might go with them on the return voyage, because they were persons well skilled in navigation.

Kubla Khan agreed, and a squadron of ships was fitted out. They sailed from China in the year 1292. Marco was now thirty-eight years old. There were many delays, and the voyage to Persia lasted two years.

When Marco Polo reached Persia, he heard that Kubla Khan had died. So the three Venetians decided not to return to China.

The young King of Persia gave them a safe conduct and a troop of mounted soldiers to protect them. Without this protection, they would have been in great danger of being killed on the way.

It was in 1295 that they finally arrived back in Venice, twenty-four years after they had left it.

They had been away so long that no one recognised them. They were dressed in the worn Tartar clothing in which they had been travelling, and they had almost forgotten how to speak Italian. Their stories of the wonders of Kubla Khan's palaces were disbelieved, and the merchants of Venice mocked them as idle vagabonds.

But the travellers were not as poor as they looked. Ripping open the seams of their shabby clothes, they produced handfuls of rich jewels.

How did the story of Marco Polo come to be written?

Either Marco had a very wonderful memory, or he kept notes of all the places he visited, because years afterwards he was able to dictate, word for word, all that is set down in his book.

This was written out by a man who was a prisoner in Genoa, where Marco Polo was also imprisoned for three years. Both had been captured by the Genoese in a sea fight between the galleys of Venice and Genoa.

Marco Polo, who had commanded one of the Venetian galleys, returned to Venice for the second time in 1299. His adventures were over.

We know nothing more about him. But his book remains, to give us a wonderful picture of the teeming life of the East, and to make his name for ever remembered as one of the most remarkable travellers of all time.

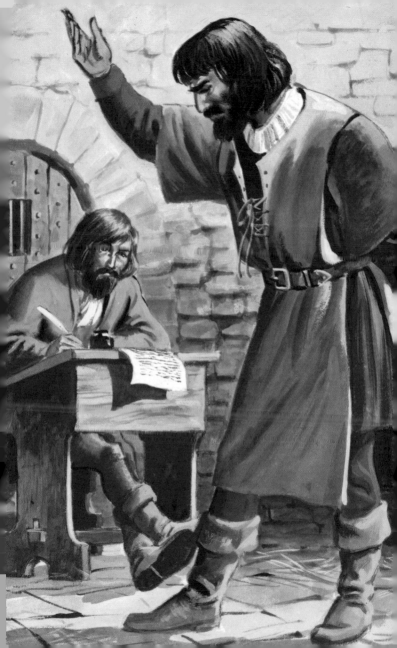

EUROPE

Genoa
Venice

Sudak

BLACK SEA

Constantinople

Layas

Acre

Jerusalem

MEDITERRANEAN
SEA

Baku

CASPIAN SEA

PERSIA

Baghdad

PERSIAN GULF

Kerman

Ormuz

Bokhara

Samarka

Ba

Kab

The TRAVELS of MARCO POLO